A NOTE TO PARENTS

When your children are ready to "step into reading," giving them the right books—and lots of them—is as crucial as giving them the right food to eat. **Step into Reading Books** present exciting stories and information reinforced with lively, colorful illustrations that make learning to read fun, satisfying, and worthwhile. They are priced so that acquiring an entire library of them is affordable. And they are beginning readers with an important difference—they're written on four levels.

Step 1 Books, with their very large type and extremely simple vocabulary, have been created for the very youngest readers. **Step 2 Books** are both longer and slightly more difficult. **Step 3 Books,** written to mid-second-grade reading levels, are for the child who has acquired even greater reading skills. **Step 4 Books** offer exciting nonfiction for the increasingly proficient reader.

Children develop at different ages. **Step into Reading Books,** with their four levels of reading, are designed to help children become good—and interested—readers *faster*. The grade levels assigned to the four steps—preschool through grade 1 for Step 1, grades 1 through 3 for Step 2, grades 2 and 3 for Step 3, and grades 2 through 4 for Step 4—are intended only as guides. Some children move through all four steps very rapidly; others climb the steps over a period of several years. These books will help your child "step into reading" in style!

Random House 🏠 New York

Text copyright © 1995 by Dayle Ann Dodds.
Illustrations copyright © 1995 by Matt Novak.
All rights reserved under International and Pan-American Copyright Conventions.
Published in the United States by Random House, Inc., New York, and simultane-
ously in Canada by Random House of Canada Limited, Toronto.

Library of Congress Cataloging-in-Publication Data
Dodds, Dayle Ann.
Ghost and Pete / by Dayle Ann Dodds ; illustrated by Matt Novak.
p.   cm. — (Step into reading. A Step 2 book)
SUMMARY: Pete and his new friend Ghost go trick-or-treating on Halloween, but
Ghost can't remember what to say.
ISBN 0-679-86199-8 (pbk.) — ISBN 0-679-96199-2 (lib. bdg.)
[1. Ghosts—Fiction.   2. Halloween—Fiction.   3. Friendship—Fiction.]   I. Novak,
Matt, ill.   II. Title.   III. Series: Step into reading.   Step 2 book.
PZ7.D66285Gh   1995
[E]—dc20   94-43102

Manufactured in the United States of America   10 9 8 7 6 5 4 3 2 1

STEP INTO READING is a trademark of Random House, Inc.

GHOST
and
Pete

A Step 2 Book

By Dayle Ann Dodds
Illustrated by Matt Novak

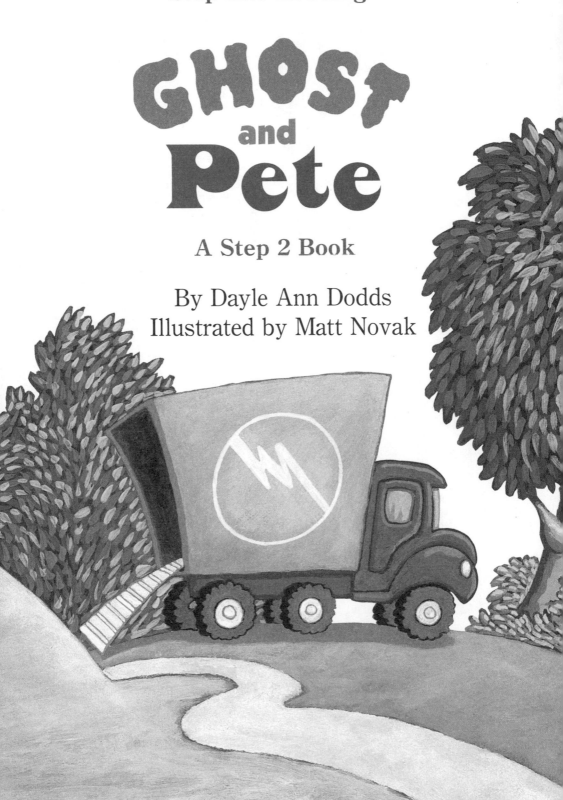

"Here is our new house!" said Pete.

Pete ran downstairs.

He ran upstairs.

He found more stairs.

They went up—

up to the attic.

Pete looked around.

He saw spiderwebs.

He saw old hats.

He saw old shoes.

He saw old boxes—

and one of them was moving.

"YEOW!" Pete cried.

The box wiggled.

It moved back and forth.

It stopped, and made a noise.

Mmmmm, went the box.

"It could be a kitten,

stuck in the box," Pete thought.

Pete opened the lid.

He peeked in.

Two eyes looked at him.

It was NOT a kitten.

"AHHHH!" screamed Pete.

"AHHHH!" screamed Ghost.

Pete shut the lid.

His heart went THUMP THUMP.

Pete sat down on the box.

Now that thing—that ghost—

was shut in the box.

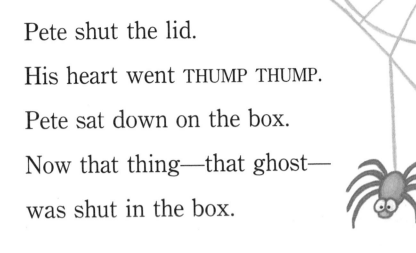

It was quiet for a minute.

Then Pete heard someone crying.

SNIFF, SNIFF.

That made Pete feel sad.

He opened the box.

"What is wrong?" Pete asked.

"You scared me," said Ghost.

"You scared *me,*" said Pete.

"I have never seen a ghost before."

"Please let me out," said Ghost.

"I have been in this box a long time."

"How long?" asked Pete.

"One hundred years," said Ghost.

Ghost flew out of the box.

Ghost was not tall.

Ghost was not wide.

Ghost was just like Pete.

"What did you do in the box

for a hundred years?"

Pete asked.

"I sang," said Ghost.

"You must know a lot of songs,"

said Pete.

"Just one," said Ghost.

"It is called

How Many Toes Does

a Skeleton Have?

It goes like this:

How many toes does a skeleton have?

Ten. Sing it again."

Pete heard his mother.

"Pete!" she called.

"Time for lunch!"

"I have to go," Pete said.

Ghost looked sad.

"But I will come back," said Pete.

Ghost looked happy.

"I am very good at waiting," said Ghost.

"I will see you after lunch."

Pete came back after lunch.

"Ghost? Where are you?" he said.

Pete looked all around the attic.

Then he heard a noise.

It came from the box.

"What are you doing
  back in the box?"
  Pete asked.
"I am used to it," said Ghost.
"Come with me," said Pete.
"You can see my new room."

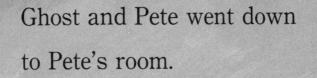

Ghost and Pete went down
to Pete's room.

"Do you like it?" said Pete.

"Yes," said Ghost.

"It is full of boxes.
I feel right at home."

CLOTHES
PLANES
PUZZLES
TOYS
SHOES
BOOKS
GAMES
SHOES
TRAINS
TOYS

Ghost looked at each box.

One said BOOKS.

One said PUZZLES.

One said GAMES.

One said CARS AND TRUCKS.

But one box did not say anything.

"What is in *this* box?" Ghost asked.

Pete smiled.

"A ghost," he said.

He opened the box.

He took something out.

It was white.

It had two holes.

"That is not a ghost!" said Ghost.

"I am a ghost, and I don't look

like that at all."

"Turn around
and close your eyes," said Pete.
Ghost turned around.
He closed his eyes.

"Are you peeking?" Pete asked.
"Oh, no," Ghost said.
"Ghosts never peek."

"Look at me!" Pete said.

Ghost turned and looked at Pete.

"You are a ghost!" Ghost said.

"Just like me!

Why didn't you say so?"

"I am not really a ghost," said Pete.

"This is my costume for Halloween.

We will go trick-or-treating tonight.

We will get candy.

I will be a ghost.

And you can be—"

Pete looked in the box.

He found something else.

It was yellow, orange, and blue.

It had feathers and a beak.

It had a tail.

"You can be this!" Pete said.

"You want me to be a chicken?"

Ghost asked.

"Not a chicken," said Pete.

"A parrot. Try it on.

You can wear a mask.

You can say: Trick or treat.

And you can get candy.

It will be fun."

"Trick or treat," Ghost said.

"I can do that.

And I love candy.

Okay, Pete—let's go!"

Pete put on his costume.

He looked like a ghost.

Ghost put on his costume.

He looked like a parrot.

Ghost and Pete went to the first house.

Pete rang the bell.

A lady opened the door.

"GIVE US CANDY!" Ghost shouted.

"You are a loud little bird," the lady said.

She was not smiling.

Then she shut the door.

"She did not give us candy!" Ghost said.

"You must be nice," said Pete.

"Now try again."

They went to the second house.

Pete rang the bell.

"Now say something nice,"

Pete said to Ghost.

A man came to the door.

"Trick or treat," said Pete.

"I like your mask," said Ghost.

"That is my face,"

said the man.

He was not smiling

either.

The man shut the door.

"Pete," said Ghost.

"I am not very good at this."

"Let's try again," said Pete.

"This time, don't say a word."

"I can do that," said Ghost.

They went to the third house.

Pete rang the bell.

"Hello, children," the lady said.

"Would you like some candy?"

"Yes, thank you," said Pete.

He took a cherry lollipop.

The lady looked at Ghost.

"Would *you* like some candy?"
the lady asked.

Ghost did not say a word.

"I said, WOULD YOU LIKE
SOME CANDY?" the lady asked again.

Ghost did not say a word.

"I guess not," the lady said.

"Good-bye."

She shut the door.

Ghost looked sad.

"Come," said Pete. "We will get you
a piece of candy this time."
They went to the fourth house.

Pete rang the bell.

"Just say yes,"

Pete told Ghost.

A little girl answered the door.

She had a basket full of candy.

She was dressed like an angel.

She had sparkly wings.

She had a halo.

"Have you ever seen a prettier angel than me?" the little girl asked.

"Yes," said Ghost.

SLAM went the door.

"Let's go home," said Pete.

Pete and Ghost went home.

Pete put on his blue pajamas.

He brushed his teeth.

He put his lollipop on the table
by the bed.

Ghost put on Pete's red pajamas.

Pete and Ghost climbed into bed.

Pete turned out the light.

It was quiet.

It was dark.

Pete heard a noise.

It went SNIFF, SNIFF.

Pete picked up his lollipop.

He gave it to Ghost.

"Happy Halloween, Ghost," said Pete.

"I am glad you are my friend."

"I am glad too," said Ghost.

"Good night, Ghost," said Pete.

"Good night, Pete," said Ghost.

Pete closed his eyes.

He heard someone singing

very, very quietly.

"How many toes does a skeleton have?

Ten. Sing it again."

Pete smiled,

and then he fell asleep.